POSTMODERN ENCOUNTERS

Darwin and Fundamentalism

Merryl Wyn Davies

Series editor: Richard Appignanesi

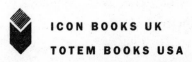

ICON BOOKS UK

TOTEM BOOKS USA

Published in the UK in 2000
by Icon Books Ltd., Grange Road,
Duxford, Cambridge CB2 4QF
email: info@iconbooks.co.uk
www.iconbooks.co.uk

Published in the USA in 2001
by Totem Books
Inquiries to: Icon Books Ltd.,
Grange Road, Duxford,
Cambridge CB2 4QF, UK

Distributed in the UK, Europe,
Canada, South Africa and Asia
by the Penguin Group:
Penguin Books Ltd.,
27 Wrights Lane,
London W8 5TZ

In the United States,
distributed to the trade by
National Book Network Inc.,
4720 Boston Way, Lanham,
Maryland 20706

Published in Australia in 2001
by Allen & Unwin Pty. Ltd.,
PO Box 8500, 9 Atchison Street,
St. Leonards, NSW 2065

Library of Congress catalog
card number applied for

Series editor: Richard Appignanesi

ISBN 1 84046 177 2

Typesetting by Wayzgoose

Printed and bound in the UK by
Cox & Wyman Ltd., Reading

Creation vs. Evolution?

In August 1999, the state Board of Education of Kansas in the United States voted by a narrow margin to permit the removal of evolution from the teaching curriculum. This was not an isolated case. In thirteen American states, from California to Maine, there have been challenges to the teaching of evolution. In some states the demand is for equal treatment for the burgeoning field of creation science (see 'Key Concepts' at the end of this book), the scientific inquiry to substantiate the King James Bible account of creation contained in the Book of Genesis. Alabama requires a disclaimer to be printed on the front of biology and geology textbooks, stating that evolution 'is theory not fact'. Illinois has put evolution in the category of 'controversial issues', allowing local school districts to decide for themselves how the subject will be taught. Organised challenges to Darwin are not confined to the classrooms. The Internet carries hundreds of sites devoted to partisan controversy over the means, meaning and import of creation vs. evolution.

The current battle between Creationists and

Evolutionists is presented, in the media and by scientists, as a rerun of the initial controversies that greeted the publication of Charles Darwin's *On the Origin of Species* in 1859. Darwin's theory of evolution, transformation and adaptation within the course of time was a watershed in intellectual history. It has become a basic premise of our common understanding. Yet, for many people it is not the ultimate answer to everything. In particular, evolution attracts the wrath of Christian fundamentalists. But are the Christian fundamentalists the only people who question Darwin and evolution? Is the battle between evolution and fundamentalism a battle between the light of reason and the darkness of dogma? Is science really being persecuted by religion? The angry rhetoric and impassioned fight over public policy places Darwin on a par with Galileo, constantly raising the spectre of the Inquisition.[1] Is this a realistic perception? Can scientists be as fundamentalist as their Christian opponents? Can we recognise a scientific fundamentalism that operates in the same manner as Christian fundamentalism? If we cannot – why not?

We have become comfortable with the idea that this clash of Christian fundamentalism and Darwinism is the real nub of the debate between religion and science. Darwin, Darwinism and Darwinistic thought are different viewpoints as much within science as between science and Christian fundamentalists. To see these concerns as affecting only Christian fundamentalists is to marginalise and silence a diversity of moderate but equally pertinent positions. A true appreciation of the historic context of Darwin, the socially constructed nature of science, and theologically and historically informed understanding of religion, which is much more than simply Christian fundamentalism, suggests that we are being hijacked by two extremist positions. The legitimate questions about the relationship between science and religion, what it is reasonable to believe as science and as religion, are not just obscured but rendered inarticulate by two radical, partisan misconstructions.

It is simplistic to begin at the beginning. In this debate, that is how all the problems arise. Science as evolution, as well as Christian fundamentalism, comes to origin and creation with a clear context and agenda. So let's begin with this agenda.

Western Agenda before Darwin

The publication of *On the Origin of Species* is presented as a moment of revolutionary overthrow. From that moment on, one either believed in evolution or continued to believe in the no longer tenable notion that God created the world on 23 October 4004 BC. Notice how this familiar construct is already a Hobson's choice – no choice at all. The trouble is that that is not what happened at all.

The date of Creation, 4004 BC, was inserted into the margin of all editions of the authorised King James Bible from 1701. The date was established by backtracking Biblical chronology from known and dateable events. It was the work of the Archbishop of Armagh, James Ussher (1581–1656) in his book *The Annals of the World*. In his day, Ussher was regarded as one of the leading scholars in Europe. He was a bibliophile, amassing a great collection of books and manuscripts that became the foundation of the library at

Trinity College, Dublin, established by his uncle, also named James Ussher. The pertinent question is why Ussher should undertake such a task, involving considerable research and mental dexterity. In what context, what intellectual climate, did such a question come to require such precise reasoning?

In Western civilisation, the Bible is a basic source of all understanding. A synthesis of Christianity and the knowledge of the ancients, the Greeks and Romans, had been made by the Church Fathers in the early centuries of Christianity. Portions of this knowledge were preserved through medieval times; considerably more was recovered during the passion for classicism we call the Renaissance. Contrary to the general impression, the great consequence of this new emphasis on classical texts was not humanistic art but mercantile endeavour and religious reform. Basing himself on the erroneous small-earth calculations of Ptolemy, newly republished in the mid-15th century, Christopher Columbus argued it was possible to reach the fabled riches of the East by sailing west. He made landfall on a peopled continent unknown to the Church Fathers or the Ancients, the Americas. Within a generation of Columbus's voyage – from 1492 to 1512 – study of early Greek religious manuscripts prompted Martin Luther to reformulate the concept of Christianity with momentous implications for European society. These two wellsprings meant that the entire accepted framework for understanding the origin and purposes of Creation, life, the universe and everything had to be answered anew. Out of the reformed religious idea of reason and the rational accumulation of knowledge made possible by exploration and travel, modern science as we know it developed.

It was rationalism, in the Age of Reason, that prompted Bishop Ussher to meticulous calculation. A new sense of time and its meaning had become a matter of vital interest. When Europe became aware of the ancient civilisations of India and China, their lengthy recorded history led to speculation that they were older than Hebrew civilisation, a matter of no small concern. The Old Testament is, in one sense, an historical document. The first five books, the Pentateuch, believed to be written by Moses, include the account of the Creation, the origin of all humanity – from Adam and Eve and then as Noah's progeny after the Flood – the basic explanation for the dispersion of all peoples and diversity of human culture and society – the consequence of the fall of the Tower of Babel. These conceptual and historic referents were the means for rationalising and reasoning with human nature, culture, society and all human institutions, not only for religious creed and doctrine but also for natural philosophy. If India and China, so different from the West, were earlier and more original in history, the entire edifice of what was known and thought was in jeopardy. The Darwinian moment, the confrontation with the unthinkable, has a long history in Western experience. Darwin's onslaught, if onslaught it was, was not unique.

The Hebrew people, the original source of humanity by virtue of the Bible account, gave a genealogical conception of the unity of mankind as a species. It was both the authority of Scripture and the conception of mankind that turned on the question of dating, the matter of time. Bishop

Ussher's conclusions have become notorious, but he was not the only ardent calculator. Isaac Newton spent a great deal of his eminent career preoccupied with Biblical chronology for exactly the same reason as Ussher, to exactly the same end, to re-establish orthodoxy by confirming the historic primacy of the Hebrew people of the Biblical account. The *philosophes* of the Enlightenment were also interested in the question. Voltaire, an advocate of the superiority of Chinese civilisation – both moral and historical – became an instant convert to India as the seedbed of humanity when he acquired an ancient Hindu manuscript. Unfortunately, this ancient Veda was a forgery produced by Voltaire's arch-enemies, the Jesuits.[2]

The argument about time, chronology as an urgent matter of interest, opened the floodgates in many ways. The Genesis account came under scrutiny and became a matter of controversy that is with us even today. The problem was a continent previously neither suspected nor mentioned. Where did its people come from? Were they real human beings with souls? These questions affected political claims to territory and the legal rights of European monarchs to dispose of people. Victory for the best interpretation, human unity, permitted them to be made serfs tied to European masters. It was also a vital matter for the natural philosophy of human nature. Numerous eminent thinkers began to question the Biblical Flood and subject the Genesis account to critical scrutiny. Isaac de la Préyère (1594–1676) argued against a universal Flood, in favour of it being a local phenomenon.[3] From this, along with Paracelsus and Bruno, he went on to suggest not one but at least two creative episodes as far as mankind was concerned. Monogenesis, the idea of a common origin of all mankind, was and remains the dominant idea, as fundamental to Darwinism as to Christian thought. But polygenesis has been a persistent idea, reformulated in various guises at various times to support racial theories. The Bering Straits theory of the peopling of the Americas originated early to explain and locate Amerindians within the overall construct of unitary humanity, dispersed, like everyone else, at the fall of the Tower of Babel. Amerindians were offshoots of the peoples of Asia. This remains archaeological orthodoxy despite the logical, chronological and evidentiary difficulties it imposes.[4]

The intellectual ferment of the Age of Reconnaissance and Reformation refashioned the idea of time in another fundamental sense. Chronology became intimately connected to the idea of human adaptation, development and change. The concepts of degeneration and progress arrived early, deeply implicated in the new understanding of the proper meaning and interpretation of Genesis. Reports of the radically different lifeways of the inhabitants of the Americas and other regions newly visited provided a way to think of the past as being unlike the present. A new imagery was given to the old ideas of savagery and barbarism, which derive from the Greek and always signify a person lacking in reason. Suddenly, American Indians were the image of Ancient Britons. The importance of reason in Reformation thought propelled the idea of savage barbarism as a prelude to the providential rise of civilisation. Developmental stages of human civilisation, a unitary process of adapta-

tion and change, became central to the social
thought of the Enlightenment. The medieval idea
of hierarchy within Creation, the 'great chain of
being', led seamlessly to the idea of hierarchy in
human history, demonstrated by living relics, the
savage and barbarous societies identified around
the globe, the living fossils of human degeneration or stalled, static evidence of earlier eras of
progress. The meaning of time was reforged.
Transitional forms in the hierarchy of living
beings also entered the scheme of thought.
Linnaeus included humans with tails, Africans
and Amerindians as such a transitional category
between the apes and mankind proper. The
French anthropologist Gobineau, aided by
Buffon, who advocated the historical view of life,
planned an active search for living man-apes.[5] So
the idea of the *primitive*, the concept of a virtually
bestial condition of early human existence, was
alive and thriving long before Darwin and evolution. It had been rationalised as a consequence of
modifications in understanding Genesis, com-
monly accepted, invoked and refashioned by generations of thinkers. Chronology and racism have

been potent partners in the history of ideas about human origins.

Science and natural philosophy, political and social thought in Western civilisation, have always been cross-fertilised. Concepts and their meanings have a history, a history of ideas; they have been subject to revision and change. Thinkers need ideas as substance to reason with, and the substance has always had a great deal to do with religion, in the sense of Biblical concepts and ideas. The central idea around which modern science developed, the concept of a mechanical universe, became the ruling orthodoxy. It originated with Newton and Descartes. Both developed their concept of the universe the better to comprehend and integrate their religious ideas with their science. It was the central purpose of reformed religion founded on reason to understand the other book of God, the natural world, without resort to miracles and direct continuous intervention of the Divine. Our concept of the laws of nature, more often today called the laws of physics, is a direct lineal offspring of this intellectual imperative. Descartes' formulation of matter and mind was intended as a synthesis, one that established and located the sacred/spiritual within a mechanistic natural order. Religion and science are not perpetual enemies; they have been closely related kin in the history of ideas. The ideas of time and its meaning, deployed by so many thinkers before Darwin, created the context that enabled his theory of evolution to be assimilated with continued Christian beliefs. Old reductive orthodoxies, the young earth creationist position, did not disappear – human ideas are intensely retentive – but their persistence does not mean that they are the only tenable ideas or the only ones that occupy intellectual space within religion or society, or science.

Darwin's Origins

Charles Robert Darwin was born in 1809, the second son of a successful and wealthy physician, Robert Waring Darwin. His grandfather, Erasmus Darwin, also a physician, was internationally known for his poetic descriptions of the natural world. In *Zoonomia; or The Laws of Organic Life*, his verse epic, Erasmus Darwin introduced the idea of evolution. Charles's mother was a daughter of Josiah Wedgwood, founder of the famous pottery, an active supporter of the intellectual life of his times that linked him not only to Erasmus Darwin but also to Joseph Priestley, the famous chemist. From both sides of his heredity, Charles Darwin was linked to the old Unitarian and radical tradition. Old radicalism gave way to popular religious revival and led on to the muscular Christianity we associate with the public face of the Victorian heyday. Technology continued to change the face of industrialising society, and natural science became a fashionable interest for gentlemen. Throughout his adult career, Darwin lived on the income from investments while he pursued his career in natural science.

Young Charles Darwin disliked his medical studies in Edinburgh. He took a greater interest in geology. After leaving Edinburgh he enrolled at Cambridge to prepare for the life of a cleric. He studied classics, divinity and maths at Christ's College and attended lectures on biology. He was an ardent bug collector. After going down from Cambridge he accompanied Adam Sedgwick,

Professor of Geology at the university, on a momentous summer expedition to study the geology of North Wales. In 1831 Darwin, through the recommendation of friends, got the position of naturalist on HMS *Beagle*'s voyage to chart the coasts of South America and the South Sea Islands. On this five-year mission, Darwin assiduously collected specimens of natural fauna, noted geological formations and fossils and visited the Galapagos Islands.

On his return to England in 1836, he began to work on establishing his scientific credentials. Ill health led him to retreat from a public life in science. He removed to the quiet of Down House in Kent in 1841 and from there he patiently continued his researches. Darwin opened his first notebook on the transmutation of species in 1837. His first reasonably comprehensive outline of the theory of natural selection was written just before the move to Down House. In 1844 he wrote a 230-page essay covering the topics dealt with in *Origin*, leaving instructions with his wife that it was to be published in the event of his untimely death.

By 1856, Darwin was being encouraged by his closest associates to publish his ideas. He had completed ten chapters when in 1858 he received a paper written by Alfred Russel Wallace, a young naturalist working in Borneo, containing his independently conceived idea of natural selection. Joint papers were read at a hastily assembled meeting of the Linnaean Society, including an extract from a letter by Darwin to the American botanist Asa Gray, as proof of Darwin's claim to chronological priority on the idea. Darwin then completed *Origin of Species*. It was published on 24 November 1859 and sold out on the first day.

Darwin's career is a subject of heated debate about ways of understanding science and scientists. Are scientists lonely seekers after Truth, observing, measuring, testing, experimenting and driven to conclusion only by facts? Or are scientists, while observing, measuring and testing, involved in and products of the social construction of knowledge, influenced by the society in which they live and its ideas, ideas that shape the questions asked and answers given to problems in science? In which case, scientists are in an active sense inventors rather than passive discoverers, imposing a pattern informed by many strands of cultural influence on phenomena they study. The growth of the Darwin industry, the study of the enormous volumes of his correspondence and writings, mean it is possible to see how he worked, what he read, what influences he acknowledged.

Darwin pursued meticulous researches on corals, barnacles, domesticated animals, corresponded with animal breeders – pigeons were of particular interest. There was a great deal of biological investigation. From the quiet life of seclusion in Kent, Darwin was in active correspondence with all the leading names in science, and gradually began cultivating those who would be influential in the acceptance and success of his ideas. He was, in contemporary terms, a superb networker. He followed a systematic programme of reading that made him well-versed in the intellectual currents of his time.

Darwin himself acknowledges his debt to Malthus in conceiving the idea of natural selection. In his D notebook of September 1838, Darwin first refers to the political philosopher and parson T.R. Malthus, and his *Essay on the Principle of Population*. As Bowler has observed: 'There can be little doubt that in the end the concept of the "struggle for existence" described by Malthus played a major role in switching his thoughts onto the path that led towards natural selection.'[6] Or as Darwin himself wrote: 'Towards the close I first thought of selection owing to struggle.'[7] Malthus's book was preoccupied with the Poor Law and the burden on society of a growing population of the poor, whose numbers increase geometrically while the food supply increases only arithmetically. Malthus refers to the struggle for existence when discussing competition among primitive tribes, harking back to the old Hobbesian ideas of the 'nasty, brutish and short' life of the savage. Wallace also credited this same source with sparking his own ideas on natural selection. In 1855 Darwin notes that he considered his ideas on natural selection as analogous to the 'division of labour'; we know that he also read Adam Smith's *Wealth of Nations*.

Influence does not mean lack of originality or creative thinking. Darwin took the metaphor of the struggle for life from Malthus and made of it something that was not in Malthus at all, i.e., struggle as a *creative* process by weeding out the unfit in every generation. The creative aspects of Darwin's thought were, however, impelled by ideas about human society in a context where social thought was, and had long been, developmental, adaptive and deeply wedded to the concept of arising from primitive form.

We know Darwin was immensely concerned about the reception of his ideas, designing his structure and form of argument to make it acceptable. In this he succeeded to a very large degree. The best illustration of this is Herbert Spencer, the social philosopher, author of *Social Statistics* – 'an attempt to strengthen laissez faire with the imperatives of biology'[8] – published in 1851. He was the acme of social evolutionary thought, an active part of the network promoting Darwin's ideas. Spencer adds another important strand to the social construction of knowledge thesis: that Darwin and his ideas were many things to many people. Spencer disproves the idea that publication of *Origin* was a Hobson's choice for religious ideas. Far from propelling people to abandon God the Creator, Darwin's natural selection is a unitary explanation of all life, infused with 'the social values so beloved of middle class mid-Victorians living in the heyday of laissez faire capitalism'.[9] It is presented replete with hooks that enabled it to be grafted onto a long extant intellectual tradition. Evolution was a newly articulated law of nature, like all the other laws promulgated by the Creator and left to work accordingly. The survival of the fittest, a phrase coined by Spencer,[10] expressed an intensely Victorian view of the old idea of providence leading to the rise of civilisation. And Spencer insisted that religion and science could be reconciled, now and for all time; 'the Unknowable' was 'inviolable'.[11] The extended title of *Origin – Or the Preservation of Favoured Races in the Struggle for Life* – had an obvious resonance for how Western civilisation understood itself, its history and current activity, the civilising, colonial mission of the fittest. When later Darwinians, especially

Thomas Henry Huxley, sought to emphasise a materialist interpretation of Darwin, Spencer became a lukewarm Darwinian.

For all those like Spencer who could synthesise evolution with Christian belief and ideas, a group that ranged from Wallace to J.D. Rockefeller,[12] there were others who would not or could not. Some rejected Darwin's theory because they saw its inevitable consequence as a materialist view of existence. We know this was the viewpoint of Adam Sedgwick, who had opened the world of geological time to Darwin. The famous debate between Huxley and Wilberforce, the Bishop of Oxford, centred on an explicitly creationist view of the origin of species. There was also much detailed criticism of whether Darwin had in fact made a cogent and acceptable scientific theory, whether or not that threw Christian belief into question. Perhaps the most telling antidote to hagiography and the mythic view of Darwin is to consider his end. Darwin died in 1882, 23 years after the publication of *Origin*, and a mere nine years after the publication of *The Descent of Man*. A campaign was immediately started, with support from

19 Members of Parliament, and quickly succeeded in gaining permission from the Dean of Westminster for Charles Darwin to be buried in Westminster Abbey, close to Newton and Faraday. Not usually the fate of a scurrilous controversialist who had overthrown established religion.

The Theory of Natural Selection

On the Origin of Species By Means of Natural Selection is the grand theory of the age of grand theories. As Darwin himself expressed it, it was a theory about all organisms throughout all time 'by which all living and extinct beings are united by complex, radiating and circuitous lines of affinities into one grand system'.[13] Darwin took the analogy of a tree to symbolise his vision:

The green and budding twigs may represent existing species. At each period of growth, all the growing twigs have tried to branch out and on all sides, and to overtop and kill the surrounding twigs and branches, in the same manner as species and groups of species have tried to overmaster other species in the great battle for life.[14]

Establishing the argument for natural selection began by pointing to artificial selection, the kind engaged in by the pigeon fancier and stockbreeder. Working on the variation naturally and randomly occurring within species, better breeds are produced. Natural selection also works on these variations in the wild, in context of the struggle for existence where more organisms are born than can survive and reproduce. Those better adapted, fitter, are more likely to survive and leave more offspring. Where Malthus used the metaphor of struggle for existence in relation to collective activity, that of tribes, Darwin saw the struggle taking place at the level of the individual: 'individuals having any advantage, however slight over others, would have the best chance of surviving and of procreating . . . On the other hand, we may feel sure that any variation in the least degree injurious would be rigidly destroyed'.[15] A secondary mechanism, sexual selection, is added to the struggle for food and survival. In sexual selection, the struggle is for mates and reproductive success. Natural selection means increase in frequency of those best adapted, their characteristics spread through a whole population, until the average character of a species changes. All life is genealogically connected by the process of 'descent with modification'. Small changes that are continually underway, it is assumed, will eventually add up to give the major developments, the appearance of new forms of life.

To accommodate his theory, Darwin needed huge amounts of geological time to permit natural selection to operate and to house the fossil record of this evolutionary process. His discussion of the geological record, despite the acknowledged gaps, points out that more general and linking forms are found lower, hence earlier, in the fossil record, with more specialised forms higher and hence later. Life never moves back on itself. Natural selection occurs within geographic distribution across specific environments. The fitter survivors are those best adapted to take advantage of their environment:

From the war of nature, from famine and death, the most exalted object which we are capable of conceiving, namely, the production of the higher animals, directly follows. There is a grandeur in this view of life, with its several powers, having been originally breathed into a few forms or into one; and that, whilst this planet has gone cycling on according to the fixed law of gravity, from so simple a beginning endless forms most beautiful and most wonderful have been, and are being evolved.[16]

A grand unifying theory obviously had to include mankind. As Gruber and Barrett point out: 'The subject of man and his place in nature was so woven into Darwin's thought that it forms an indispensable part of the nature of his beliefs.'[17] The first passage in the Darwin notebooks that clearly enunciates the idea of natural selection and applies it to man was written on 27 November 1838. In another of his notebooks, Darwin noted, 'I will never allow that because there is a chasm between man . . . and animals that man has a different origin'.[18] What Darwin would not allow he took a very long time to get around to saying. 'Light will be thrown on the origin of man and his history', Darwin had written in *Origin*.[19] Both the intensely Christian Charles

Lyell (*Antiquity of Man*, 1863) and Huxley (*Man's Place in Nature*, 1863) published before Darwin. *The Descent of Man* could have been no surprise when it was finally published.

Darwin left plenty of scope for those who would interpret natural selection as theistic evolutionism, creationism: 'As natural selection works solely by and for the good of each being, all corporeal and mental endowments will tend to progress towards perfection.'[20] Intellectual adjustment, reasoning along this line, had been underway since the Reformation. Experts argue vociferously whether Darwin himself remained a believer or not. Maybe he did, maybe he did not. Most likely, he devolved into a vestigial agnosticism. Darwin explicitly defended the idea that evolution by natural selection did not have an intentional design, which would invoke the old idea of creation by design that his entire theory sought to replace. But he very clearly inserted and permitted the upward escalator idea of progress that had long been the understanding of God's providential purpose in the creation of natural law. His imagery of nature, 'red in tooth and claw', could nevertheless be understood as all being for the best in the best of all possible worlds.

Origin went through many revisions. The first edition concluded with the likely objections to the theory; subsequent revisions dealt with the arguments raised after publication. And problems there were. Darwin established a theory, but in numerous instances, he had not solved problems. Natural selection succeeded because it provided a general framework of assumptions, an overview, a means of approaching problems and asking questions. The vital issue of how heredity operated to provide the variation by which natural selection worked was not so much a 'black box' as something Darwin got wrong. He knew nothing of genetics – his idea of 'gemmules' did not convince contemporaries and has been completely overtaken by genetics. It is possible to go to *Origin* and identify specific errors or points that later work has proved inadequate. But that is not quite the point. The lasting significance of Darwin is the use to which his work and reputation have been applied by later generations. As Peter Bowler has observed:

Darwin's theory was created from the study of small scale changes in the modern world, it concentrated on explaining the actual processes that still affect every living thing, not the reconstruction of long past evolutionary links – and thus ignored what many contemporaries saw as the most important questions in the study of progress in life on earth.[21]

The important questions of Darwin's day lead on to the controversies of today. In all the permutations of evidence brought forth and argued, natural selection is the credo determinedly clung to by all scientific opinion. Darwin is invoked and called in defence by all shades of opinion and interpretation because his is such a grand theory, such a permissible structure, whatever perspective one takes on the actual evidence. And natural selection has another utility for science:

In the end the success of Darwinism rested not on the exploitation of the selection theory but on the exploitation of evolutionism by those who were

*determined to establish science as a new source of
authority in western civilisation.*[22]

Darwin and his theory of natural selection are
much more than a specific scientific theory, they
are icons of power and territory, cultural icons
about the appropriate order and superiority of
sources of explanatory power. That is why scientists find such useful and willing helpmates in
creationists.

The Scopes Monkey Trial

The decision of the Kansas Board of Education is
the latest round in an ongoing, surrogate tussle
over the authority of science. The politicised
arena of legal and public policy was not the
immediate response to Darwin. It is a cultural
phenomenon of 20th-century America, a response
to the consequences of Darwinism. The 1920s
were a period of rapid social and technological
change. The American population was immensely
altered by immigration in the preceding decades.
Assimilating them into the ethos and ideas of
America was invented in the early 20th century.

In cinema, radio and other media, it involved nostalgia that solidified an American tradition. Protestant religion, an essential and prominent part of the American tradition, is founded on scriptural study and routinely prone to enthusiastic revivalism. This is the context in which 36 bills were introduced in 20 states during the 1920s, all seeking to ban the teaching of evolution in public schools. In Tennessee, the Butler Act made it unlawful 'to teach any theory that denies the story of Divine Creation of man as taught in the Bible, and to teach instead that man has descended from a lower order of animals'. John Butler, a member of the state legislature, said he proposed the act after hearing a preacher tell of a young woman who returned from university believing in evolution and disbelieving in God.[23] The Butler Act was passed in 1925. The Governor of Tennessee said: 'Nobody believes that it is going to be an active statute.'

It became active because of teacher John Scopes and his trial at Dayton, Tennessee – the infamous Monkey Trial. The trial is now a cultural icon about values: the values of science and free-speech liberalism as the modern understanding of the American Tradition – as against fundamentalist religion and narrow prejudice that were its unfortunate historical antecedents. The interpretation exists independent of and often quite contrary to the events.

The Monkey Trial did not happen because John Scopes had been imprisoned for violation of the Butler Act, which had no such provision, its maximum penalty being a $100 fine. It occurred because the American Civil Liberties Union (ACLU) wanted to test the statute, and a citizen of Dayton, George W. Rappelyea, was keen to put his town on the map. Rappelyea saw an advertisement in a Chattanooga newspaper seeking a teacher willing to take the Butler Act to court, all expenses paid, and persuaded a reluctant Scopes to agree. The ACLU was duly notified: 'Professor J. T. Scopes, teacher of science Rhea County high school, will be arrested and charged with teaching evolution.' Scopes, however, was not a science teacher. He had majored in pre-law and had never actually taught evolution. He had filled in during the illness of the biology teacher for two weeks at the end of the school year. Normally he taught maths and was the football coach.

The trial began on 10 July 1925, and attracted national attention amid a circus atmosphere. It was the first trial to be covered by a national radio broadcast and to receive international coverage, thanks to the 65 telegraph operators who sent daily reports over the newly-laid transatlantic cable. A show trial in all senses of the term ensued. And what a show – the trial turned on the 'single-handed combat' of the principal lawyers: 'Darrow, the apostle of knowledge and tolerance, and Bryan, the arch advocate of ignorance and bigotry.'[24] These duellists were the distinguished liberal lawyer Clarence Darrow and the populist Democrat politician, William Jennings Bryan, a former Secretary of State and failed Presidential candidate.

Notoriety became canonical when the trial was fictionalised in the Broadway play *Inherit the Wind* by Jerome Lawrence and Robert E. Lee, first produced in 1955. It was translated to the screen in 1960 when the Clarence Darrow character acquired the venerable, kindly common sense screen persona of Spencer Tracy. The multiply-produced *Inherit the Wind* has entered into the culture as most people's concept of the Scopes Trial. Play and film are faithful to the courtroom 'single-handed combat'; indeed, no drama could surpass the reality, yet both are simplified and reductive representations of the ideas that occupy the testimony.

The defence's stated purpose was to set before the jury 'what value to progress and comfort is the theory of evolution'. They intended to show 'that the book of Genesis is in part a hymn, in part an allegory and work of religious interpretation by men who believed the earth was flat and whose authority cannot be accepted to control the teachings of science in our schools . . . that the Bible is a work of religious aspiration and rules of conduct which must be kept in the field of theology . . . that there is no more justification for imposing the conflicting views of the Bible on courses of biology than there would be for imposing the views of biologists on a course of comparative religion'.[25]

The defence defined the problem and articulated

exactly the problematic nature of the relationship between religion and science that bedevils a secular society in which religion continues to inform the views of many citizens. Today, the 'unjustified', in Darrow's terms – imposing biological constructs on religion as the only explanation of its origin and meaning – is commonplace. From fundamentalist geneticists of the selfish gene variety to sociobiologists and evolutionary psychologists, this is a basic article of faith. It is certainly implicated in the rise of the current backlash of fundamentalist religion.[26] The Scopes trial is rightly, but often for the wrong reasons, seen as a single-handed combat for the authority of science against the stranglehold of religion, where religion is defined as only one particular creed.

The denouement of the trial, and its fictionalised forms, came when Clarence Darrow called William Jennings Bryan as a witness. After insisting that a 'Read Your Bible' banner be removed from the courthouse, Darrow's cross-examination began. Bryan stated: 'I believe everything in the Bible should be accepted as it is given there: some of the Bible is given illustratively.' Darrow inquired whether this meant Bryan believed that Jonah was swallowed by the whale – the answer to which is that the Bible does not mention a whale, but a big fish. The question of time and Bishop Ussher was raised, Darrow posing the old familiar question: 'How many people were there in China 5,000 years ago?', and then getting down to specifics:

Q. *Would you say that the earth was only 4,000 years old?*

A. Oh no, I think it's much older than that.

Q. *Do you think the earth was made in six days?*

A. Not six days of twenty-four hours.

Q. *Doesn't it say so?*

A. No sir . . .

Q. *'The morning and the evening of the second day' mean anything to you?*

A. I do not think it necessarily means a twenty-four hour day.

Q. *What do you consider it to be?*

A. I have not attempted to explain it. If you will take the second chapter – the fourth verse of the second chapter says: 'These are the generations of the heavens and of the earth, when they were created in the day that the Lord God made the earth and the heavens'; the word 'day' there in the very next chapter is used to describe a period. I do not see that there is any necessity for construing the words, 'the evening and the morning' as meaning necessarily a twenty-four hour day, 'in the day when the Lord made the heaven and the earth'.

Q. *You think those were not literal days?*

A. I do not think they were twenty-four hour days. [. . .]

Q. *You do not think that?*

A. No. But I think it would be just as easy for the kind of God we believe in to make the earth in six days as in six years or in 6,000,000 or in 600,000,000 years. I do not believe it is important whether we believe one or the other.[27]

This extract is not the usual précis of testimony, not exactly the version included in *Inherit the Wind*. Apocryphally, Bryan walked straight into Darrow's trap by denying young earth creationism – which is hardly a proof of evolution, and clearly not a position Bryan espoused or was particularly seeking to defend. To take the Monkey Trial only in its most reduced 'free speech and liberty against religious bigotry' perspective is to invite the consequences that have followed.

Bryan put into evidence the basic Christian, indeed religious, concept of God. It informs all religious positions, and can lead to a variety of responses to evolution, including critical questioning that is valid, reasonable and pertinent. Such a concept explains why, even if Genesis is 'part hymn, in part an allegory', mankind is distinct from the rest of creation, even if both evolved. Mankind alone is capable of conceiving of its own creation, of receiving Divinely inspired teaching or revelation, and by virtue of these special conditions acknowledging 'religious aspiration and rules of conduct' in all circumstances, even in the operation and actions of science. The religious argument is not about assertions of science, in the narrow sense of whether they are accurate or inaccurate, but about the purposes and ends of such knowledge, how it is acquired and used. From a religious perspective there is a moral and ethical dimension to everything, including science; nothing is value-free or neutral, everything is accountable. Evolution *per se* is irrelevant to that argument, unless it is argued intentionally by science that by virtue of evolution man is a purely material being. Not all those who embraced Darwin's theory interpreted it as materialist. In the 20th century such interpretation has become both more prominent and more aggressive. The argument is made that genes are the only determining programme of all living things. Genes have become an alternative 'moral code', our only source of 'rules of conduct'. What drives and determines life is the genetic imperative to survive and reproduce at the expense of everything else. It is not just Christian fundamentalists, whose conception of religion causes them to question whether this is good science and good natural philosophy, who had a right to be worried where Darwinian thinking would lead. The Scopes Trial was not the end of the argument. It signals issues that people are still anxious to debate outside a circus atmosphere.

The religious issues at the heart of the Scopes Trial underpin present-day debates. If science is a god – a humanly-produced source of ultimate authority – those whose lives it affects demand greater responsibility and accountability from science. The defence team, at various points in the Monkey Trial, stated their desire to harmonise the positions of the contending parties – an objective still desired by the vast majority of the American public.[28] If there has been no reconciliation, it is as much the responsibility of the *Inherit the Wind* syndrome, invoked by creationist-baiting scientists, as it is of extreme 'young earth' creationists.

Creation Science

The outcome of the Scopes Trial was a technical draw. Scopes was found guilty and fined by the judge. On appeal, the conviction was thrown out on the technicality that the fine should have been left to the jury. Despite being projected as a vindication for evolution, in the aftermath more statutes based on the Butler Act were passed. In Tennessee it lingered long, and though never again invoked, it was not repealed until 1967. The following year, Arkansas teacher Susan Epperson sought to test her state's anti-evolution law, passed in 1928. The United States Supreme Court found the statute unconstitutional on the grounds that the First Amendment does not permit a state to require that teaching and learning must be tailored to the principles or prohibitions of any particular religious sect or doctrine.

The 60s were an era of change, of rising living standards, the dawn of consumer abundance. In the United States it was the era of civil rights reform and anti-war demonstrations. The radical movement sought to sweep away outmoded attitudes and enhance personal freedom. Cults and consciousness-raising are what we associate with the 60s, and California was the place where it was all happening. Other things were also going on in California of a rather different nature. The space – inner spiritual, social and legal – that was being sought for personal redefinition opened new avenues for Christian fundamentalists as well. The money-raising facility of conservative Christians is legendary. Old-style tent revivalism moved with the times; it colonised television and radio and enabled new organisations to get active and involved. As the Creation-Science Research Center observes in a review of its first 25 years:

In 1964, members of our staff were involved in the writing of the Civil Rights Act, reinserting the protection of creed in the public sector against offence to religious belief and the reaffirmation of that wording in the new civil rights act covering all public funds.

In 1970, The Creation-Science Research Center was formed in order to introduce Creation-Science as a balance in science education under these guidelines.[29]

Christian fundamentalists have become activists, highly professional and proficient advocates of their creed. Only the inflexible tradition of perceiving Christian fundamentalists as simple-minded bigots prevents people appreciating how sophisticated, subtle and adept they have become in utilising changing circumstances to mount their campaign. Their activism, and the strategic gains they seek to make, have been moulded and reshaped by the cultural, political and legal climate of the times that gives them access to decision-making and constrains their operation. More importantly, they formulate their arguments in terms of the sociology of knowledge, which argues that all science is socially constructed, and that postmodern thought has doubt as an essential premise. To this is added a large measure of Socratic questions and answers which guides discussion to the desired conclusion. They publish textbooks and popular tomes, operate research institutes, seek to rewrite curricula, and love to engage evolutionary scientists in acrimonious and infuriatingly redundant disputes.

Bishop Ussher is back on the agenda, but the particular endeavour that occupies them is making distinctions that create thorny philosophical and intellectual knots for postmodern reasoning. Ironically, these fundamentalists emphasise postmodern relativity about all grand narratives and argue that science is just one among a collection of grand narratives. Their terminology, the language of creation science, projects a scholarly inquiry that by contemporary criteria cannot be denied its appropriate place in the science class.

According to Henry M. Morris, founder and President Emeritus of the San Diego-based Institute of Creation Research, there are three questions that should be treated as separate scientific issues in public education: 1) Special creation versus naturalistic evolution as the ultimate explanation of the universe, life and man; 2) Age of the earth; 'ancient earth' versus 'young earth'; 3) Uniformitarianism versus catastrophism (including not only intermittent local catastrophism, but also a global cataclysm) as the basic framework of interpretation in earth history.[30] Morris is the doyen of the field. Along with John Whitcomb, Jr., he wrote *The Genesis Flood* (1961), the opening blast of the modern reformulation of creationism. Creation science, it is argued, is distinct from Biblical Creation, which is not its necessary meaning or purpose. Creation science is devoted to scientific inquiry of basic evidences for creation and against evolution. It concerns such matters as gaps in the fossil record, the laws of thermodynamics, the complexity of living systems and any other anomalies they can allude to in the ongoing business of science. Creation scientists, many of whom, we are told, were formerly evolutionists, are convinced by scientific evidences, not by faith, that scientific data explicitly supports the Creation Model and contradicts the Evolution Model. This assertion stands on another prop – the argument that neither creation nor evolution is testable, in the sense of being experimentally observable. They make a fundamental distinction between fact-based science and process-based science, by which they mean science perceived through over-arching paradigms. Take science, they argue, as a search for truth: wherever that search leads we should go, provided we can create a level playing field for inquiry. It is surely possible that a Creator exists, and cannot scientifically be disproved, so it is at least possible that creation is the true explanation of the origin of our intricately complex universe. Therefore, it is inexcusable 'to arbitrarily exclude even the consideration of special creation as a scientific model from public institutions, when it might well be true, and therefore profoundly and perfectly scientific'.[31]

Lest this new language take us too far from our expectations, we are assured that scientific creationism is compatible with Biblical creationism, though each can be taught and evaluated separately. 'Scientific creationists are as opposed to the teaching of Biblical creationism in public school as evolutionists are', writes Morris. But what Biblical creationism, like Morris, wants is the reinstatement of good old Bishop Ussher and 4004 BC. Creationists, as scientific creationists or Biblical creationists, young earth creationists or any of the other variants, preclude Biblical exegesis in any form. The literal meaning of the Bible is its only meaning.

In *A Creationist's Defense of the King James Bible* (1996), Morris defends not only one literal meaning but also only one translation: 'One reason is that all fifty or more translators who developed the King James Bible were godly men who believed strongly in the inerrancy and full authority of Scripture and who, therefore, believed in the literal historicity of Genesis, with its record of six-day Creation and the worldwide flood. This has not been true of many who have been involved in producing the modern versions.' Science may be strategically useful as a search for truth, but textual analysis, exegesis, literary and manuscript analysis is not. What postmodernism gives it also takes away, probably to ensure balance. By this pincer approach, however, creation scientists do immense violence to God-given reason. The meaning of the Bible ends with an act of human knowledge, the translation of the King James Bible completed in 1611. The work of these translators, who are the new repository of all Biblical meaning, is valuable for the beliefs ascribed to them and interpretation imposed upon them, rather than for the text itself. It is the ultimate in reductive closure that commits exactly the same enormity, placing human thought as superior to Divine Creativity, of which evolution is supposedly guilty. By locking Biblical meaning to one specific English language translation, even if it is the most mellifluous and pleasing, Christian fundamentalists are cutting themselves off from the language in which Divine inspiration and revelation actually occurred, and from the processes of human understanding by which their own creed was founded. Had one text of the Bible and one meaning only stood for all time there could have been no Martin Luther, no Calvin and no Christian fundamentalists to exert political power in the United States of America. The Reformation urged translation of the Bible into vernacular languages to promote critical reason, not to end it.

Bible literalism is essential to creation science. Biblical creation must be anchored and fixed to distinguish it from *theistic* creationism – the more general religious viewpoint founded on the unfolding of human understanding of revealed and inspired text. The problem with theistic creationism and Biblical exegesis, as Morris has explained, is that it is not 'evangelistically fruit-ful'.[32] Any diminution of Bible literalism, he argues, suggests that the Bible is in error, when what it actually shows is that it is people now and in past history who have been and will remain prone to error. In religion, as much as in science, the search for truth must be ongoing, wherever it leads. God's truth surpasses human understanding: therefore human reason must keep on striving to comprehend what it implies.

Creation scientists are young earth creationists. They not only need Bible literalism – they need science, the fact-based kind. They are more than happy to abstract findings of science to bolster their attack on evolution. They utilise as much scientific observation, measurement and experiment as possible to pick holes in evolution and to support the old argument that complex design needs a designer – the designer being the Creator. It is a subsidiary point to demonstrate that science proves literalism. But when it comes to theory, they do not need scientific ones, but relativistic postmodernism. As Morris writes: 'The scientific method involves reproducibility, the study of present natural processes. When men attempt to interpret the events of the prehistoric past [a concept that does not exist for Bible literalists, since Genesis *is* history] or the eschatological future, they must necessarily leave the domain of true science . . . and enter the realm of faith. This faith may be in the doctrine of uniformity, which assumes that the present processes may be extrapolated indefinitely into the past or the future.' Since extrapolations are neither reproducible nor subject to scientific checking, 'the most that can be done is to argue that his [the scientist's] theories are either probable or improbable on the premise of his own uniformitarian presupposition, depending on the logical consistency of the superstructure he has erected on this foundation'. Therefore it is open to any individual to 'pretty well believe what he wants to believe. He can erect a logical system within which he can explain all the physical data upon any one of any number of mutually exclusive and contradictory premises'.[33]

A theory is whatever one wants to believe, and, according to some versions of postmodernism, one belief is as good as another. The argument for balance is a well chosen strategic device, though it has consistently met a negative response in American courts. The battle began in California in the 1960s, when creationists gained control of the State Board of Education, a position that lasted from 1963 until 1974. In 1972 they sought to include separate creation of species in biology textbooks, prompting a major campaign by scientists. A recurring pattern of court engagements has been ebbing and flowing across America ever since. For example, Seagraves vs. State of California (1981) found that the state's science framework, as written and qualified by its anti-dogmatism policy, gave sufficient accommodation to free exercise of religion. The policy provided that class discussion of origins should emphasise that scientific explanations focus on 'how', not 'ultimate cause'. Any speculative statements concerning origins in text or in class should be presented conditionally, not dogmatically. In McLean vs. Arkansas Board of Education (1989), 'balanced treatment' of creation science was held to violate the Establishment Clause of the US Constitution – it had no secular purpose, and creation science is not in fact a science. In 1987, the US Supreme Court found Louisiana's creationism act to be unconstitutional for impermissibly endorsing religion. In 1994, in Peloza vs. Capistrano School District, Peloza's definition of a 'religion' of 'evolutionism' was rejected. In 1997, a requirement that teachers read aloud a disclaimer whenever they taught evolution, ostensibly to promote 'critical thinking', was rejected by the District Court for Eastern Louisiana. 'In mandating this disclaimer, the School Board is endorsing religion by disclaiming the teaching of evolution in such a manner as to convey the message that evolution is a religious viewpoint that runs counter to . . . other religious views.' (Freiler vs. Tangipahoa Parish Board of Education) In August 1999, just as the Kansas Board of Education was taking its vote, this ruling was upheld on appeal.

Creation science has most definitely had many days in court. Kansas will no doubt provoke many more. By its activity, a specific form of creationism has appropriated a more general debate. It has been made into a private contest between scientists and Bible literalists. The common language of lay discussion in phrasing any question about evolution has been appropriated and is taken to indicate only one objective: to further the ends of a minority and their Bible literalism. It has also generated mutually held conspiracy theories: creationists see atheistic materialism lurking everywhere; scientists see any questioning of evolution as the thin end of the creationist's wedge. These private conspiracy theories silence religion as understood, and believed by, many people in America and elsewhere.

Evolution is a legitimate concern and subject for questioning by anyone – it is not capable of giving ultimate answers to all ultimate causes. Theistic evolution has been a general response to Darwin since the publication of *Origin*. More people in Kansas had questions about how science presented evolution than just Christian fundamentalists.

The state Catholic education officer, Mary Kay Culp, said: 'A major concern here is teaching evolution as a fact protected from any valid scientific criticism.'[34] She not only complained that the NAS standards, the model science curriculum rejected by the Board of Education, seemed to put 'science as a way of knowing' above religion, but it associated religion specifically with superstition and myth.

Despite all efforts by scientists to represent the fundamentalist backlash as an 'Inquisition', the Pope, indeed Popes, make it clear that the religious position is otherwise. Before the modern reformulation of Christian fundamentalism, Pope Pius XII in 1950 released the Encyclical *Humani Generis*. It 'considered the doctrine of "evolutionism" a serious hypothesis worthy of a more deeply studied investigation and reflection on par with the opposite hypothesis'.[35] It went on to state: 'For these reasons the Teaching Authority of the Church does not forbid that . . . research and discussions, take place with regard to the doctrine of evolution, in as far as it inquires into the origin of the human body as coming from pre-existent and living matter . . . However, this must be done in such a way that the reasons for both opinions, that is, those favorable and those unfavorable to evolution, be weighed and judged with the necessary seriousness, moderation and measure.' In 1996, the present Pope, John Paul II, addressing the Pontifical

Academy of Sciences, went even further. He stated: ' . . . new knowledge leads us to recognise in the theory of evolution more than a hypothesis . . . The convergence, neither sought nor fabricated, of the results of work that was conducted independently is in itself a significant argument in favour of this theory.'[36]

The essential point of Christian belief and the basis of its concern about theories of evolution is the status of the human person. Reiterating the words of *Humani Generis*, the Pope defined this as being: 'if the human body takes its origin from pre-existent matter the spiritual soul is immediately created by God.'

Pope John Paul II went on to say:

Consequently, theories of evolution which, in accordance with the philosophies inspiring them, consider the mind as emerging from the forces of living matter, or as a mere epiphenomenon of this matter, are incompatible with the truth about man, nor are they able to ground the dignity of the person. In other terms, the human individual cannot be subordinated as a pure means or pure instrument either to the species or to society.

But the experience of metaphysical knowledge, of self-awareness and self-reflection, of moral conscience, freedom, or again, of aesthetic and religious experience, falls within the competence of philosophical analysis and reflection while theology brings out its ultimate meaning according to the Creator's plans.

Scientific Fundamentalism

The complexity and sophistication of the Pope's position stands in stark contrast to Richard Dawkins's position as expressed in *The Blind Watchmaker*:

This book is written in the conviction that our own existence once presented the greatest of all mysteries, but that it is a mystery no longer because it is solved. Darwin and Wallace solved it.[37]

Using a form of words that is a mirror image of Henry Morris's own, Dawkins goes on to say:

I want to persuade the reader, not just that the Darwinian worldview happens to be true, but that it is the only known theory that could, in principle, solve the mystery of our existence. This makes it a doubly satisfying theory. A good case can be made that Darwinism is true, not just on this planet but all over the universe wherever life may be found.[38]

So both Morris and Dawkins present their truths as the only Truth.

Dawkins's absolute pan-galactic certainty is the stuff of acrimonious dispute within science itself. 'What is really at stake', according to Niles Eldredge's succinct summary, 'is two diametrically opposed suppositions about how evolutionary biology should be conducted'.[39] The opposing camps are the ultra-Darwinians, or Darwinian fundamentalists, who specialise in genetics and whose most public proponent is Richard Dawkins; and the naturalists who work in a number of fields, but especially palaeontology, and whose most published proponent is Stephen Jay Gould. The argument took shape during the

1960s and 70s. Ultra-Darwinism, whose emi-
nence is John Maynard Smith, gathers pace in
The Genetical Evolution of Social Behaviour
(1962) by William Hamilton, George Williams's
Adaptation and Natural Selection (1966), and
culminates with Dawkins's *The Selfish Gene*
(1976). The opposing view emerged with the
publication of *Punctuated Equilibria: An Alternative to Phyletic Gradualism* (1972) by Gould
and Eldredge. These two opposing strands have
taken evolution beyond the modern synthesis.

The modern synthesis of Darwinism was made
in the 1930s and 40s. It was the work of such
people as Ronald Fisher, Theodore Dobzhansky,
Ernst Mayr and J.B. Haldane. The synthesis
brought genetics firmly into the Darwinian fold.
Darwin was wrong about how heredity worked,
though heritable variation was the essential substance on which natural selection operated. The
rediscoveries of Mendelian genetics at the beginning of the 20th century were initially thought to
undermine or sideline Darwin. Genes certainly
had a powerful effect on Darwinian interpretation, not least through the enthusiastic support

that Francis Galton, Darwin's cousin, gave to *eugenics*: the idea that fitter breeds of humans could be produced intentionally. This led to the famed nature/nurture debate: are humans determined by their genetic make-up; or is humanity's great adaptive invention, culture, behaviour acquired in our diverse societies, more important in making us who and what we are? Eugenics is not a nice idea, though eminently Darwinian. Franz Boas, the founding father of modern American anthropology, organised cultural anthropology to counter eugenics. More generally, anthropology spent much of the 20th century rooting out social Darwinism, social evolutionary thought and simple determinism of various stripes to locate human nature within nurture, the realm of culture. The nature/nurture themes have been subsumed in the post-synthesis debate, in which they appear in somewhat altered but still pertinent guise. Genes were accepted as more basic, the real level of evolution, in the sense of generating mutations that initially were thought to explain the origin of species. Large-scale mutations then turned out to be more likely disastrous than sustainable. Eventually, it was found that there were ongoing, small-scale mutations that could fuel natural selection. Mathematics demonstrated that genetic characteristics working through a population would be compatible with the predictions of natural selection. The new Darwinian orthodoxy was established.

The modern synthesis has been succeeded by a 'coordinated movement' of scientists, based on a shared conviction that 'natural selection regulates everything of any importance in evolution, and that adaptation emerges as a universal result and ultimate test of selection's ubiquity'. These scientists 'push their line with an almost theological fervour', says Gould.[40] 'We have an elegantly simple theory of evolutionary change and if we are to heed the geneticists (and Darwin), we simply take the natural selection model of generation by generation change and *extrapolate* it through geological time. And that to my paleontological eyes is just not good enough. Simple extrapolation does not work', argues Eldredge.[41] The 'punctuated equilibria' thesis is based on the nature of the fossil record. Species appear in the fossil record as distinct entities. Once they appear, they tend not to change much at all. The bouts of speciation are relatively rapid, in comparison to the intervening long periods of stasis. The history of evolution, to the naturalists, is also a history of extinctions, some of which have been triggered by catastrophe. It is the naturalists, and their pluralist ideas of evolution, who are parodied by fundamentalist creationists – at least one reason which leads them to stress Darwinian orthodoxy, in the face of being charged with trying to sneak purpose back into evolution and giving aid and comfort to the fundamentalist enemy.

The naturalists evince total commitment to natural selection, though the various strands of their Darwinian pluralism consistently chip away at the edifice Darwin built. Population genetics brings evidence of the large role of neutral, and therefore non-adaptive, changes in the evolution. Developmental biologists point to 'conservation', the close similarity of basic pathways of development of different organisms. In which case, limitation, rather than adaptive honing to perfection, becomes the dominant theme of evolution.

Palaeontology requires that long-term evolutionary trends be explained as the distinctive success of some species versus others, and not as a gradual accumulation of adaptations generated by organisms within a continuously evolving population. It also shows the effect of historic contingency, the importance of catastrophes and mass extinctions, that bears little relation to evolved adaptive reasons for success of lineages in normal Darwinian times. 'Evolution includes so much more than natural selection', Gould has stated, so much more that it cannot be reduced to the fashionable, logical reductions of his evolutionary opponents. These look like incommensurate views of evolution. So why is that not even a legitimate, reasoned question? Why is it impermissible to contemplate a new paradigm beyond Darwin and insist on backtracking to alternative textual references in Darwin, who is thereby rendered true for all time, no matter what, as the scriptural authority? The naturalists may not have the 'theological fervour' of their scientific opponents, but they certainly organise themselves within the kind of theological orthodoxy familiar to religious history.

The 'ultra' in ultra-Darwinism comes from the gene-centred view of absolutely everything. The genes are for specific things: what they effect are adaptations that shape an organism's form, function and behaviour to achieve reproductive success and adaptation. It is a radically reductive view in which the idea of a species collapses. The focus of attention is on populations, a subset of a species, where gene frequencies are tracked mathematically. The genes' imperative to leave more copies of themselves to imprint on future generations is 'the heart of Darwinian biology, and the fervent, singular credo of the ultras', says Gould. The ultimate ultra is the *selfish* gene. Dawkins's highly evocative arguments take gene-centredness to its logical culmination where organisms as discrete entities disappear over the horizon.

Now they swarm in huge colonies, safe inside gigantic lumbering robots, sealed off from the outside world, communicating with it by tortuous indirect routes, manipulating it by remote control. They are in you and in me; they created us body and mind; and their preservation is the ultimate rationale for our existence. They have come a long way, those replicators. Now they go by the name of genes, and we are their survival machines.[42]

In the various constructions of gene-centred thought, genes develop agency, more consciousness and purpose than the lumbering robots that bear them. Where is it all leading? E.O. Wilson provides the answer:

What, we are compelled to ask, made the hypothalamus and limbic system? They evolved by natural selection. That simple biological statement must be pursued to explain ethics and ethical philosophers if not epistemology and epistemologists, at all depths.[43]

Biology, in the shape of our genes and their adaptationist programme, is the ultimate answer to everything. Despite biologists clearly demonstrating that there is no evidence, indeed no way to comprehend how there could be genes for specific behaviours, perhaps specific anything, we are deluged with genes determining us. Dawkins shares a common idea with sociobiology and the new replicator on the block, evolutionary psychology. The importance of genes is adaptation. Demonstrate adaptiveness, and evolution by natural selection is assured. Adaptiveness is a throwback, something that fitted us for an earlier stage of evolution. So the human brain, by which we compute behaviour, was formed in the Upper Pleistocene. We have, in short, Stone Age brains. By this fortunate conclusion, a great deal of redundant 19th-century anthropology re-enters the discourse. In formulations strikingly reminiscent of how kinship terminology and practice was explained then, what we do *today* is explained because it served the purposes of our early ancestors on the African savannah. Fortunate indeed that it did. The prehistoric void, so limited in the quantity of physical evidence from which to infer any behaviour, has always had great attractions for interpretative thinkers. It is a space where the natural progression from hypothesis to all the semantic force of the hypothetical is effortlessly transcended. Now, with all the authority of scien-

tific evolution as ultimate explanation, this space
– our environment of evolutionary adaptiveness –
is where genes for spite, aggression, xenophobia,
indoctrinability, homosexuality and the charac-.
teristic difference between men and women first
learned what was fittest. It is also the place where
humanity originated as a genocidal being.[44]

Conclusion

How do we ground the dignity of the person at
the dawn of the third millennium? Dignity is
something we all seek and value. Our sense of
dignity derives from our sources of meaning.
Despite what scientists may tell us, science has
become an unlimited inquiry into meaning.
Scientific explanation reaches into all domains;
it does not confine itself to reportage of technical detail, observing, testing and measuring.
Scientific theories build world pictures that sys-
tematise, predict and have explanatory power.
Meaning attaches to explanatory power by
invoking and employing the repertoire of ideas of
natural philosophy in the diversity and richness it
has achieved in the history of thought. In a world

where science rules, where science is consulted and justifies our choices and selection of action in business, health, education, environment, food, housing, heating – indeed, everything – the intelligent citizen must question the meanings advanced by science and its theories, for they affect the quality of our most intimate daily life. The distance between the world picture of a theory and the dignity of the human person is short, and all too persuasive for those who would claim to know best what scientific meaning determines for our fate.

Science that asserts by the most inexact of circumstantial evidence – the kind no court of law would put before a jury as reasonable inference – that we began as a 'genocidal species', is doing one of two things. Either it is reading the gross brutalities of the 20th century into our past, or producing theories that excuse the vileness of the present. What are the two opposing views of evolution offering as the dignity of the human person? Dawkins is explicit: we are lumbering robots, built body and mind by genes: 'DNA neither knows nor cares. DNA just is. And we dance to the music.'[45] Dawkins may maintain he believes that genes make us but do not compel us, yet his 'giddying updraughts of rhetoric' are repeatedly and passionately defended by their author; they persuasively convey meaning. The meaning is radical reductionism in which culture evaporates and the valuable principles that order it, self-awareness and self-reflection, moral conscience and freedom, can exist and have cogent form only if they can be extrapolated from an evolutionary process reductively construed. Darwinian fundamentalism and the progeny it has spawned should upset everyone, not just Christian fundamentalists, but anyone with the faculty of conscientious reason. A world made by the scientific imprimatur of such ideas is one where conscientious reason is marked for extinction.

Stephen Jay Gould has done battle with radical reductionism, this Darwinian fundamentalism, deploying beguiling wit, erudition and cultural acumen. What does Darwinian pluralism make of the dignity of the person, what alternate vision are we offered? Life, in all its forms and diversity, is a contingent accident of history, neither progressive nor predictable. Gould insists on seeking to dethrone the human-centred view of life – it is not for mankind. And if life has a meaning, then its meaning is bacteria, the most successful, resilient and enduring form of life. We have radical materialism as meaning: 'the radicalism of natural selection lies in its power to dethrone some of the deepest and most traditional comforts of Western thought.'[46] He quite rightly points out, as religions have also said, that 'the answers to moral questions cannot be found in nature's factuality'. In society, where science wields and protects authority, scientific facts affect directly how moral and ethical questions are answered. If nature's 'factuality' tells us nothing, then nothing is all there is to be told. There is neither rationale nor vision, except the thoughts that occur to us when we wake up in the morning – and that is the primitive consciousness that would be equally acceptable to Darwinian fundamentalists. Again, these ideas should upset everyone with a conscience.

The battle is not with Darwin; it is with the authority invested in and ascribed to Darwin, with the interpreters of Darwin. The battle has

been joined most publicly by Christian fundamentalists, who, however, have done battle only
for their own narrow, reductive and special purposes. But if either Darwin's interpreters or his
opponents silence, marginalise and effectively
prevent legitimate, reasoned questioning, then
everyone, as well as everything, that we hold dear
and need to establish is diminished – be that religion or science. Instead of a battle, there should
be informed, general debate; instead of bigotry,
religious or scientific, we need critical dialogue
that can see beyond mythic stereotypes that
propel the wrong ideas for the wrong reasons.

Notes

1. For example, see Preston Cloud's 'Scientific Creationism – A New Inquisition Brewing?', *The Humanist*, 37 (1977) pp. 6–15.

2. For discussion of the ideas of the time, see P. G. Marshall, *The British Discovery of Hinduism in the Eighteenth Century* (Cambridge: Cambridge University Press, 1970).

3. For discussion of the many ideas that occupied the intellectual climate of Préyère and Bishop Ussher, see Margaret Hodgen, *Early Anthropology in the Sixteenth and Seventeenth Centuries* (Philadelphia: University of Philadelphia Press, 1964).

4. For an interesting discussion of these issues in the context of the contemporary evolution debate, see Vine Deloria, Jr., *Red Earth White Lies: Native Americans and the Myth of Scientific Facts* (New York: Scribner, 1995).

5. For discussion of racialist anthropology in the pre-Darwinian period, see George Stocking, Jr., *Race, Culture and Evolution: Essays in the History of Anthropology* (Chicago: University of Chicago Press, 1982).

6. Peter J. Bowler, *Charles Darwin, The Man and His Influence* (Cambridge: Cambridge University Press, 1990), pp. 82ff.

7. Quoted, ibid., p. 82.

8. Richard Hofstadter, *Social Darwinism in American Thought* (Boston, 1955). Extract reprinted in *Darwin, A Norton Critical Edition*, ed. Philip Appleman (New York:

Norton, 1970), pp. 389–99.

9. Bowler, op. cit., p. 8.

10. 'A Theory of Population, Deduced from the General Law of Animal Fertility', *Westminster Review* LVII (1852), pp. 468–501.

11. The argument is made in Spencer's *First Principles of a New Philosophy* (London, 1861).

12. 'Successful business entrepreneurs apparently accepted almost by instinct the Darwinian terminology which seemed to portray the conditions of their existence.' Hofstadter, op. cit.; he also quotes an extract from a Sunday school address by J.D. Rockefeller.

13. *On the Origin of Species* (London, 1859), reprinted (Cambridge, Massachusetts: Harvard University Press, 1964), pp. 456ff.

14. Ibid., pp. 129–30.

15. Ibid., pp. 80–1.

16. Ibid., p. 490.

17. H.E. Gruber and P.H. Barrett, *Darwin on Man* (New York: Dutton, 1974), p. 10.

18. Ibid., p. 252.

19. *Origin*, op. cit., p. 488.

20. Ibid., pp. 488–9.

21. Bowler, op. cit., p. 138.

22. Ibid., p. 140.

23. Marcet Haldeman-Julius, *Clarence Darrow's Two Great Trials*, pamphlet published 1927.

24. Ibid. See extract on University of Missouri Kansas

City School of Law website: http://www.law.umkc.edu.

25. Day 4 of the trial transcript. A comprehensive website, including transcripts and supporting materials, is maintained by University of Missouri Kansas City School of Law. The site can be found at http://www.law.umkc.edu/faculty/projects.

26. Phillip Johnson, Berkeley professor of law, active disputant but not a young earth creationist, credits reading Richard Dawkins's *The Blind Watchmaker* with prompting him to enter the controversy.

27. Day 7 of trial transcript; see note 25 above.

28. In response to the Kansas vote, DYG Inc. conducted an opinion poll among American adults, sponsored by People for the American Way. They found that 83% supported the teaching of evolution in public schools. More importantly, they found that 70% believed that evolution and creation science could be harmonised.

29. Creation-Science Research Center: Twenty-five Years of Progress 1962–1987, from website: http://www.parentcompany.com/csrc.

30. Henry M. Morris, *Creation and its Critics: Answers to Common Questions and Criticisms on the Creation Movement* (San Diego: Creation Life Publishers, 1982). (Much of Morris's writing is available on the ICR website: http://www.icr.org.)

31. Ibid.

32. Morris, 'The Bible Is a Textbook of Science', in *Bibliotheca Sacra*, Oct.–Dec. 1964, available on website

listed in note 29.

33. Ibid.

34. Quoted in Edward Larson and Larry Witham's article, 'Inherit an Ill Wind', in *The Nation*, 1999.

35. Encyclical *Humani Generis*, AAS 42, 1950, p. 575.

36. Message to the Pontifical Academy of Sciences, 22 October 1996. Official translation published in *L'Observatore Romano* (weekly edition in English), 30 October 1996.

37. Richard Dawkins, *The Blind Watchmaker* (London: Penguin, 1988), p. i.

38. Ibid., p. xiv.

39. Niles Eldredge, *Reinventing Darwin: The Great Evolutionary Debate* (London: Phoenix, 1996), p. 2.

40. Stephen Jay Gould, 'Darwinian Fundamentalism', *New York Review of Books*, 12 June 1997.

41. Eldredge, op. cit., p. 3.

42. Richard Dawkins, *The Selfish Gene* (Oxford: Oxford University Press, 1976), pp. 19–20.

43. E. O. Wilson, *Sociobiology: The New Synthesis* (Cambridge, Massachusetts: Harvard University Press, 1975).

44. See article by Robert McKie, 'Light on man's dark past', *Observer*, 13 February 2000.

45. Richard Dawkins, *River Out of Eden* (London: Weidenfeld and Nicolson, 1995), p. 133.

46. Gould, op. cit.

Further Reading

Appleman, Philip, ed. *Darwin, A Norton Critical Edition*. New York: Norton, 1970.

Bowler, Peter J. *Charles Darwin, The Man and his Influence*. Cambridge: Cambridge University Press, 1990.

Darwin, Charles. *On the Origin of Species by Means of Natural Selection: Or the Preservation of Favoured Races in the Struggle for Life*. London, 1859. Reprinted Cambridge, Massachusetts: Harvard University Press, 1964.

_____. *The Descent of Man and Selection in Relation to Sex*. London: John Murray, 1871.

Dawkins, R. *The Selfish Gene*. Oxford: Oxford University Press, 1976.

_____. *The Blind Watchmaker*. London: Penguin, 1988.

Desmond, Adrian, and Moore, James. *Darwin*. London: Penguin, 1991.

Dobzhansky, T. *Genetics and the Origin of Species*. New York: Columbia University Press, 1937.

Eldredge, Niles. *Reinventing Darwin: The Great Evolutionary Debate*. London: Phoenix, 1995.

Gould, Stephen Jay. *Wonderful Life: The Burgess Shale and the Nature of History*. London: Penguin, 1959.

Gould, Stephen Jay, and Lewontin, R. 'The Spandrels of San Marco', *Proceedings of the Royal Society B*, Vol.

205 (1979), pp. 581–98.

Jones, Steve. *Almost Like A Whale*. London: Doubleday, 1999.

Lewontin, Richard. *The Doctrine of DNA*. London: Penguin, 1993.

Pinker, Stephen. *How the Mind Works*. London: Allen Lane, 1997.

Rose, Stephen; Kamin, Leon J., and Lewontin, Richard. *Not in Our Genes*. London: Penguin, 1984.

Tooby, John; Barkow, Jerome H., and Cosmides, Leda. *The Adapted Mind*. Oxford: Oxford University Press, 1995.

Wilson, E. O. *Sociobiology: The New Synthesis*. Cambridge, Massachusetts: Harvard University Press, 1978.

Key Concepts

Adaptationist Programme

The dominant expression of **Darwinian fundamentalism** today. Derives from the radical gene-centred view of evolution whereby selfish genes are the active agents competing to produce adaptations, and adaptations are the motor and proof of natural selection's ubiquity. It includes the idea that there are genes for specific things that generate the form, function and behaviour of organisms. This strand of thought leads on to sociobiology and evolutionary psychology that study human beings and society as adaptive responses to human evolution. Their crucial idea is the environment of evolutionary adaptiveness (EEA) located in the Upper Pleistocene period or Old Stone Age, when basic human adaptations are said to have developed.

Creation Science

Originated in the 1960s by a group of American fundamentalist Christians. Their research basically consists of scrutinising the work of scientists for anomalies or any material, no matter how abstruse, that either supports their belief in the literal interpretation of **Biblical creation** as presented in Genesis Chapter 1, or can be used to embarrass evolutionary scientists. They run numerous websites and publish prolifically. They also now run numerous schools and colleges in the US and are a growing force in Australia.

Darwinism

Darwin's theory of evolution is accepted by all scientists, but has led to many different strands of thought, all of which are claimed to be Darwinism. It provides the dominant paradigm within which have developed different approaches to biology, palaeontology, ecology, genetics and, in some cases, anthropology. **Neo-Darwinism** is the reaction to the rediscovery of Mendelian genetics at the beginning of the 20th century. It led to the **modern synthesis** formulated in the 1930s and 40s that integrated genetics with natural selection. **Social Darwinism** was the enthusiastic embrace of the terminology of evolution and the survival of the fittest by 19th century society. In fact, it had been in existence before Darwin, but his theory was so successful as Grand Theory that it has become associated with all the expressions of social hierarchy, progress, racial supremacy and the political and social ideas associated with them.

Fundamentalism

At some level most ideas generate fundamentalists, believers in a basic set of doctrines that are taken to be authoritative, canonical sources. **Christian fundamentalists** hold to the literal interpretation of the Bible, and for English-speaking Christian fundamentalists, that means the King James Version of the Bible of 1611, even though that is no longer the predominant translation used by

Christians. **Scientific fundamentalists** believe science to be the absolute Truth and the only way of knowing. **Darwinian fundamentalists** believe that their theory, developed under the aegis of Darwin's theory of natural selection, is the only means to conduct biology. Their approach is gene-centred, mathematical, and focused on changing gene frequencies within populations, a subset of species. It also involves the application of game theory to mathematical genetics. The results are then extrapolated through time to give a predictive model of evolution.

Natural selection

The mechanism by which evolution occurs. Natural selection is the filter for all the processes identified with evolution, universally acknowledged by all varieties and shades of scientific opinion. It includes the concepts of struggle for life, descent with modification, sexual selection, adaptation, and survival of the fittest, all generated because more offspring are produced than can survive to breed. The survivors pass on their advantageous characteristics to the next generation. Generation by generation, the character of the population would change in adapting to changes in the environment. The accumulation of this ongoing change would, over a long period of time, give rise to new species.